DATE DUE			
SE 15 97	US		
DEC 1 9 2018			

8242

534
FRI

Friedhoffer, Robert.

Sound

**SEYMOUR SCHOOL MEDIA CENTER
EAST GRANBY, CT 06026**

SOUND
BOOK 4

SCIENTIFIC MAGIC SERIES

SOUND
BOOK 4

by Robert Friedhoffer

Magical effect illustrations
by Richard Kaufman

All other illustrations
by Linda Eisenberg

Photographs
by Timothy White

FRANKLIN WATTS
NEW YORK ◆ CHICAGO
LONDON ◆ TORONTO ◆ SYDNEY

Library of Congress Cataloging-in-Publication Data

Sound / by Robert Friedhoffer ; magic effect illustrations by
Richard Kaufman ; other illustrations by Linda Eisenberg ;
photographs by Timothy White.
  p.   cm. — (Scientific magic series; bk. 4)
Includes bibliographical references and index.
Summary: Experiments, magic tricks, and other activities explore
the scientific principles of sound.
ISBN 0-531-11083-4
1. Sound—Experiments—Juvenile literature. 2. Sound-waves—
Experiments—Juvenile literature. 3. Hearing—Experiments—
Juvenile literature. [1. Sound—Experiments. 2. Experiments.
3. Scientific recreations. 4. Magic tricks.] I. Kaufman, Richard,
  ill. II. Eisenberg, Linda, ill. III. White, Timothy, ill.
IV. Title. V. Series: Friedhoffer, Robert.
Scientific magic series; bk. 4.
QC225.5.F75 1992
534'.078—dc20   92-16961 CIP AC

Text copyright © 1992 by Robert Friedhoffer
Magical effect illustrations copyright © 1992 by Richard Kaufman
All other illustrations copyright © 1992 by Linda Eisenberg
Photographs copyright © 1992 by Timothy White
Cover photograph copyright © 1992 by Timothy White
All of the manufacturing rights and sale rights for this book's original
tricks, props, and routines, as well as professional performance rights
for all items found in this book, remain the sole property of
Robert M. Friedhoffer.

Printed in the United States of America
6 5 4 3 2 1

CONTENTS

INTRODUCTION   15
   What Is Sound?   21
VIBRATIONS   23
   Experiment 1   23
   Betcha 1   24
   Trick 1—Toothpick Pulse Meter   25
   Betcha 2   26
   Experiment 2   27
WAVES   29
   Experiment 3   30
Sound Waves   31
   Experiment 4   32
   Betcha 3   34
   Experiment 5   36
   Trick 2—"Break" Your Nose   37
   Betcha 4   38
HEARING OR SOUND PERCEPTION   41
   Experiment 6   42
   Trick 3—Three Matchbox Monte   43
   Trick 4—A Nasty Gag   44
Controlling Sound Dispersal   45
   Experiment 7   46

Speed of Sound	47
Breaking the Sound Barrier	50
Effect of Temperature on Sound	52
Echoes	54
Experiment 8	54
Experiment 9	55
Sonar	56
Continuous Waves	57
Experiment 10	58
Wavelength and Frequency	58
Acoustics	59
Experiment 11	59
Experiment 12	60
Trick 5—The Messed-Up Answering Machine	61
Silent Sounds	62
The Doppler Effect	64
Loudness	64
Sound Quality	68
Indoor Acoustics	68
Standing Waves	70
Experiment 13	70
Experiment 14	71
Stringed Instruments	72
Experiment 15	73
Wind Instruments	75
Experiment 16	76
Experiment 17	78
Resonance	80
Experiment 18	80
Betcha 5	82
Forced Vibrations	83
Trick 6—The Empty Music Box	84
Trick 7—The Sound Master	85
SUPPLIERS	87
FOR FURTHER READING	90
INDEX	91

To the Helfands:
Sidney, Bernice, Jeff, Marcia, Jackie,
Scott, and Diane, in general,
and Lonnie Helfand, in particular,
a friend whose encouragement and
help made this series possible

ALSO BY
ROBERT FRIEDHOFFER

HOW TO HAUNT A HOUSE FOR HALLOWEEN

MAGIC TRICKS, SCIENCE FACTS

MORE MAGIC TRICKS, SCIENCE FACTS

SCIENTIFIC MAGIC SERIES

    MATTER AND ENERGY — BOOK 1

    FORCES, MOTION, AND ENERGY — BOOK 2

    MOLECULES AND HEAT — BOOK 3

    SOUND — BOOK 4

    LIGHT — BOOK 5

    MAGNETISM AND ELECTRICITY — BOOK 6

ACKNOWLEDGMENTS

I would first like to thank Microsoft Corporation for providing MS Windows™ and MS Word for Windows™ and Logitech, Inc. for providing a Mouseman™ Cordless mouse and a Scanman® Model 256. The aid of these marvelous products lightened the physical chores of writing and were a joy to work with.

I would like to thank the following people for helping make this book possible by supplying ideas, encouragement, and/or inspiration: Sir Isaac Newton, Leibniz, Galileo, Otto van Guericke, John Blake, John Wilkins, René Descartes, David Brewster, Carl Stenquist, Iris Rosoff, Martin Gardner, Peter and Jackie Monticup, Scott Interante, Will Shaw, Hide Kobayashi, Tom Ladshaw, Jeff McBride, Rocco LaPenta, Barry Schmoyer, Harvey Leeds, Mr. Lucky, Steve Mark, Larry Marshal, the Maltz Family, Tina Mosetis, Tom Murrin, Scott Wolfman, Vivian Nieves, Joe Stone, Tim White, Linda Eisenberg, Richard Kaufman, Howard MacNeil, Alicia Ho White, Constantine "Gus" Philippas, Russel Ward, Laura Hughes, Gregory Redich, Jonathan Choynacki, and Julie Geller.

SOUND
BOOK 4

INTRODUCTION

Even though this series of six books doesn't have to be read consecutively, it might help the beginning magical scientist to do so. The basics of physics start in the first book. Each succeeding book builds upon the knowledge of the one before. The tricks, experiments, and betchas are in there to help you have fun and get the most that you possibly can out of each book.

When you perform the experiments, you might want to *keep a notebook or diary of all of your results*. In keeping the diary, you will be following in the footsteps of such great scientists of the world as Madame Marie Sklodowska Curie (1867–1934)—radiation; Rosalind Elsie Franklin (1920–1958)—DNA; Galileo Galilei (1564–1642)—astronomy, mathematics, and physics; and Albert Einstein (1879–1955)—theoretical physics.

The tricks are laid out with EFFECT first, to let you have an idea of what the trick is about. Next comes the PROPS section, so you'll know what "stuff" you need. Then comes the METHOD, or ROU-

TINE part, which fully explains the workings of the trick. The NOTES that are at the very end of the trick try to tie the scientific principle in with the routine.

If you want to teach the science behind the tricks, you might want to explain the workings of the experiments to your friends. If you want to be a magician, you're better off not telling your friends how the tricks work. If your friends know the secrets to the trick, there is no magic.

To become a magician, you need to know all of the secrets of magic. To learn many of the secrets, you have to know something about science. You'll learn many of the "secrets" of science in this series of books.

When you learn the science, you become the magician. You just have to learn how to present the scientific principle in a mystifying way.

If you have any science tricks of your own that you think you would like to share with others, please send them along to me in care of my publisher:

FRANKLIN WATTS
95 Madison Avenue
New York, New York 10016

Perhaps I'll have room to place your trick with your name next to it in my next science/magic book. Study hard and work hard, and the universe can be yours.

Bob Friedhoffer

"The whole of science is nothing more than a refinement of everyday thinking."
—Albert Einstein, *Out of My Later Years*

"Science is the best magic."
—Bob Friedhoffer

AN OPEN LETTER TO ALL WHO READ THIS BOOK

Greetings!
Physics—the study of matter and energy and how they affect each other—*is all around us!* Pretty scary thought, eh?

Not really. Physics doesn't have to be frightening at all. There's little that we do every day that doesn't involve physics.

Here's a list of some things that use physics: riding skateboards and bicycles, playing video games, watching TV, listening to stereos, baking a cake, cooking an egg, drawing pictures, driving a car, working on your computer, shooting an arrow, playing the piano or guitar, turning on your shower, doing magic tricks, and playing practical jokes. In other words, physics is everywhere, and it can be fun if you look at it with an open mind.

I've written this series with as light a touch as possible. I've put in very little math, and all of the EXPERIMENTS can be done at or near your home for practically no expense. Almost all of the magic tricks are done with stuff you find around the house.

When you perform the magic, remember that if you want to fool your friends, you should keep the secret to yourself. If someone wants to know, "How did you do that trick?" you can honestly say, "I did it with science—physics, to be exact."

If you wish to share any secrets with your friends, don't tell them how the tricks are done; let them read the book. They can buy it or take it out of the library. If you tell them how you do a trick and they don't have to put any effort into finding out the secret, they won't respect you or the trick.

I hope that you enjoy the books in this series, and all of the experiments, tricks, and betchas that you'll find inside.

NOTE: about the use of the metric system and English system in this book. Although the metric system is easier to use, both systems are used in this series of books. In some experiments and tricks, only metric measurements are used; in others, only the English system. In still others, both are given.

Bob Friedhoffer
aka The Madman of Magic

A Couple of Jokes

Two men worked next to each other in an automobile factory for years, riveting cars together. Every day, day in, day out, all they heard was rat-a-tat-tat, rat-a-tat-tat. One day, one turns to the other and shouts in his ear, "We've worked together for twelve years

and I've got to tell you something. If you don't stop your humming, you're going to drive me crazy."

Joke 2

First guy: "Excuse me. You have a banana in your ear."
Second guy: "What?"
First guy: "You have a banana in your ear!"
Second guy: "What?"
First guy (really angry): "You have a banana in your ear!"
Second guy: "I'm sorry, but I can't hear you. I have a banana in my ear."

WHAT IS SOUND?

The dictionary tells us that sound is:

a) the sensation or perception known through the sense of hearing;

b) mechanical energy transmitted by pressure waves that is a stimulus to hearing;
c) a disturbance in matter that can be heard;
d) mechanical energy from some form of matter that is vibrating.

These definitions sound, look, and feel great, but what do they *mean*?

This book will deal with three basics of sound: vibrations, waves, and hearing.

VIBRATIONS

Vibrations are the rapid back and forth motions of matter.

Experiment 1

APPARATUS
 a foot-long ruler
 a table

PROCEDURE
Place the ruler near the table's edge, so that 2" is resting on the tabletop and the other 10" hangs over the edge. Press down on the 2" resting on the tabletop with your left palm, keeping the ruler securely in place. With your right fingertips, bend the other end down, about 2", and let it snap back into place. The twanging up and down movements are vibrations.

You may tape the ruler in place instead of holding it down with your palm.

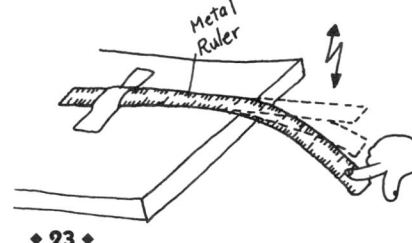

NOTE: Controlled vibrations can be very useful to us in ways that we will discuss later. Uncontrolled vibrations can be very destructive.

Betcha 1

EFFECT: "I betcha that you can't draw a straight line on top of this piece of glass with the needle on the end of the tuning fork when the tuning fork is vibrating. You can't touch the needle to anything but the glass."

PROPS

    a tuning fork (available from a music store or one of the suppliers listed in the back of this book)

    a straight pin (attached to the tuning fork with epoxy glue)

    a piece of glass that is covered with a thin smooth covering of talcum powder or soot

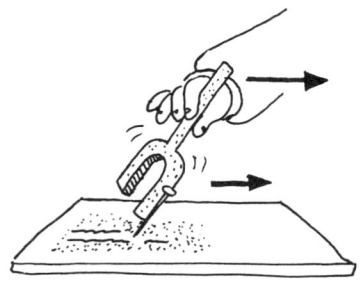

ROUTINE

The person won't be able to draw a straight line because as fast as the tuning fork is pulled across the glass, the tuning fork's vibrations will make a wave pattern in the powder.

NOTE: The vibrations of the tuning fork compress and relax the air in a rapid manner. The compression waves set up by these vibrations are interpreted by our ears as sound.

Trick 1
Toothpick Pulse Meter
EFFECT: Tell your friends that you have just gotten a new pulse meter from your doctor, and you would like to take their pulse. (The pulse is the number of times per minute that a heart beats.) You place toothpick #1 on your friend's palm, overhanging the side of the hand, and hold the end of toothpick #2 underneath the free end of toothpick #1. In just a moment, the toothpick in your friend's hand starts to jump around, just as though it's measuring the pulse rate.

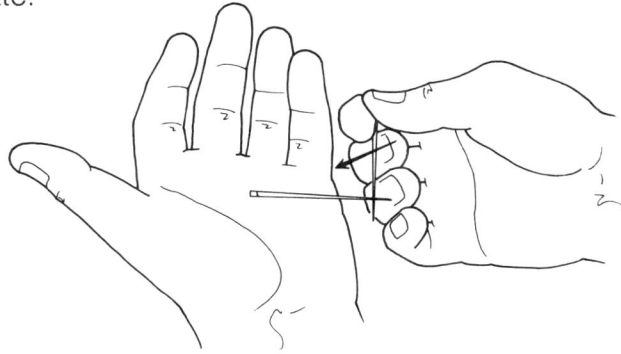

PROPS
   2 toothpicks
   a willing friend

ROUTINE
Place toothpick #1 on your friend's palm as in the illustration. Hold toothpick #2 in your right fingertips, exactly as shown in the illustration. The free ends of the toothpicks should just be touching.

Slowly, pull your right middle finger, fingernail down, keeping it tightly against the side of toothpick #2. Friction will cause it to stick a little bit, then friction will be overcome and it will slide just a little, then it will stick again, then slide, etc. This motion will be transmitted to the end of toothpick #2 as vibrations. The end of toothpick #2 will move up and down. When #2 moves up and down, it will strike the end of toothpick #1, causing it to jump up and down and look as though it were measuring your friend's pulse.

Betcha 2
EFFECT: "I betcha that I can stir this glass of water without moving my hand."

PROPS
    a glass of water
    a tuning fork

ROUTINE
Hold the tuning fork at the bottom with your right hand. Smack the tuning fork against your left palm. Place the vibrating ends of the tuning fork into the glass of water. The water will move around as if being stirred.

Experiment 2

This easy-to-make prop will show you some of the vibrations produced by your voice.

APPARATUS
- the inner cardboard core from a roll of paper towels
- a piece of tissue paper
- a rubber band

PREPARATION
Place the tissue paper over one end of the tube and secure it in place with the rubber band. Punch a small hole in the center of the tissue paper.

PROCEDURE
Stand in front of a mirror and bring the open end of the tube to your lips. All you have to do is talk into the tube. You can say anything you like, but if you

have a problem thinking of something, recite a Mother Goose rhyme. You can even hum.

Look in the mirror while you're doing this and observe the movement of the tissue paper. These movements are vibrations caused by your voice.

WAVES

WHAT IS A WAVE?

First, we'll talk about *transverse waves*. In transverse waves, the molecules of matter move up and down, at right angles (90°) to the direction in which the wave is moving. This may sound complicated, but it's not. If you tie one end of a long piece of rope to a door handle, hold on to the other end and jerk it upward, waves are formed in the rope. These are transverse waves. The molecules of rope move up and down, but never change place.

Next we have *longitudinal waves*. In longitudinal waves, the molecules move from side to side, along the direction that the wave is moving.

Now we'll talk about waves in water, just as you might find in your bathtub, a pond, a lake, or even the ocean. If you throw a stone into the middle of a still, quiet pond, circular waves will spread out from the point where the stone enters the water. The circles get larger and larger as the waves spread out. These waves are a combination of transverse and longitudinal waves. If a leaf is floating on the water's

surface, it won't move forward with the waves—it will simply bob up and down and generally stay in place.

The wave's energy is transferred forward in much the same way as the energy in the rope is transferred. As a wave will move down a rope without the rope's molecules changing relative position to each other, a wave moves through water without its molecules changing relative position.

Experiment 3
APPARATUS
    a bathtub full of warm water
    a rubber ducky or a sponge
    an understanding mom
    a couple of pennies

Run around all day and get filthy. It's O.K. Tell your mom this is another one of those real important physics experiments. Just before you're ready to take your bath, try this.

PROCEDURE
Put the rubber ducky or sponge in the middle of the bathtub. Wait until the water is calm, then drop in a penny. Look at the result. You'll see that there are circles of waves, rippling and moving away from

the place where the penny entered the water. You should also note that the duck or sponge just bobs around without moving out of place very much. This shows that the kinetic energy released when the penny hits the water is being transferred through the water in transverse waves. The water itself is not moving in the direction of the wave. You know that the water isn't moving, because the sponge and duck barely move out of place in the bathtub.

SOUND WAVES

You've seen how waves are formed and spread in water, now you'll see how they spread in air. If you go to almost any park on the Fourth of July, you're bound to see fireworks and hear the bangs of firecrackers. When a firecracker explodes, the air surrounding it is compressed, and then expands in an outward sphere, compressing the neighboring layer of air, which then expands, and so forth.

The force involved in the series of compressions and expansions is spread in much the same way as the ripples in your bathtub, except that instead of going out in circles, these "ripples" in the air move in the shape of a sphere or ball. This type of wave is called a longitudinal wave. The molecules in a longitudinal wave vibrate in the same direction in which the waves are traveling.

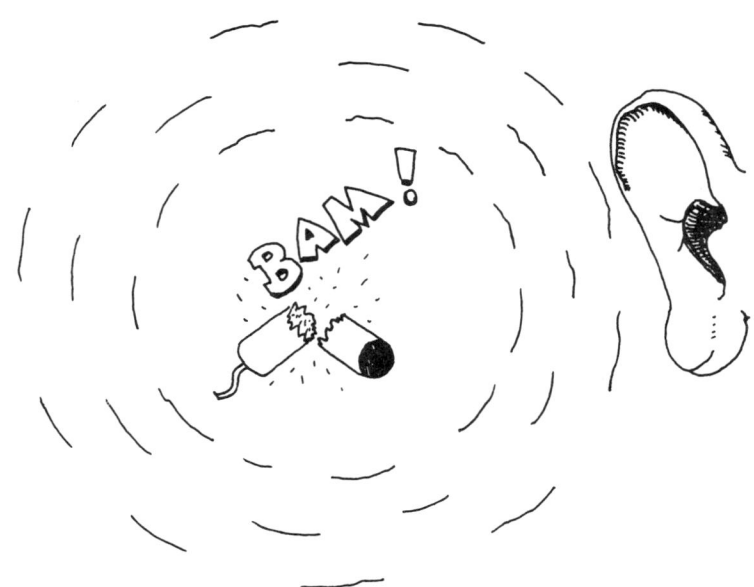

**Sphere of sound
Note: Firecrackers are dangerous.
Do not play with them.**

If you could see one sound wave spreading out, it would expand like a balloon does when it is being inflated. It starts out as a small sphere and then gets larger and larger. These sound waves are also referred to as compression waves. As the waves pass, air molecules compress, getting closer together, then expand, getting farther apart. When this compression wave hits your eardrum, it sets up a response in your body that we know as hearing.

Experiment 4
APPARATUS
  2 paper cups
  a 20-foot length of string

PREPARATION

Punch a small hole in the bottom of each paper cup. Push one end of the string into one of the holes from the bottom to the inside of one cup. Tie a knot in the end of the string so it will be securely fastened and not pull away from the cup. Do the same thing with the remaining cup and the other end of the string.

A turn-of-the-century engraving showing a tin can and string telephone

PROCEDURE

Hold onto one cup and give the other one to a friend. Have her walk away so the string is stretched fairly tight. By alternately talking into the cup, then placing the cup to your ear to listen, you can carry on a conversation with your friend.

NOTE: When you talk, your mouth forms compression waves in the air which set up waves in the cup, and then transfer to the string. The waves move down the string to the receiving cup. The receiving cup transfers the compression waves to the air contained within. The air in the cup transfers the compression wave to your ear, and your friend hears you speaking.

Betcha 3
EFFECT: "I betcha that using a string, a plastic soft drink cup, and a damp sponge, that I can make a sound like a chicken."

PROPS
    a plastic soft drink cup
    a 12-inch length of string
    a small piece of sponge, 2 inches × 2 inches

SETUP
Punch a small hole in the bottom of the cup. Push the string through the hole and tie a knot at each end of the string.

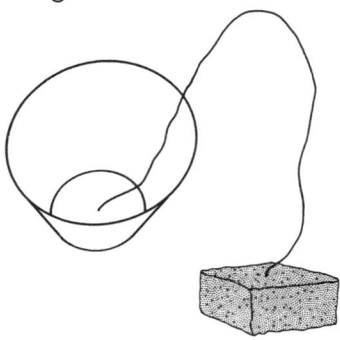

ROUTINE

Dampen the sponge. Hold the cup in one hand and fold the sponge around the string at the place where the string leaves the mouth of the cup. Squeeze the sponge with a medium amount of pressure. Pull the sponge toward the bottom of the string. A weird noise, resembling the clucking of a chicken, will come from the cup.

NOTE 1: When the damp sponge slides down the string, it will meet varying amounts of friction. It will slide easily on a smooth part, then meet greater friction and barely slide at all, then slide off that portion with a jerk to a smoother part, and so forth. When that happens, vibrations are set up in the string. These vibrations are transferred to the cup, which then transfers to the air surrounding the cup, and then to your ears.

NOTE 2: You can find a drum in well-equipped music stores that works on this same principle. Attached to the middle of the drumhead is a smooth stick that runs into the center of the drum. By dragging down on the stick with a cloth, vibrations are set up in the drumhead which then cause compression waves in the air, which our ears interpret as a sound.

Experiment 5

This experiment will let you see sound waves being made.

APPARATUS

a 15-inch stick with notches cut in it every ½ inch to 1 inch

a smooth stick

PROCEDURE

Hold the notched stick by the end in one hand and the smooth stick in the other. Rub the smooth stick over the notched stick and listen to the noise. You can go faster or slower. Each time you run the smooth stick over a notch, you create a sound wave.

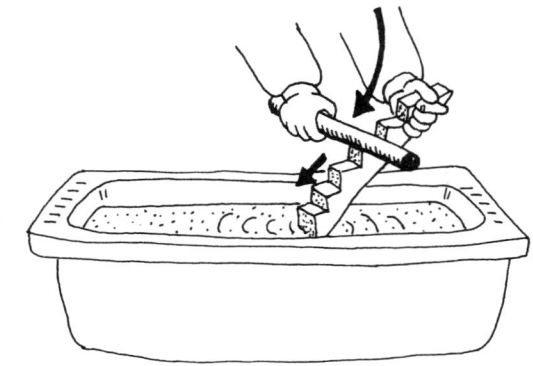

Now fill a washbasin or sink with water. Hold one end of the notched stick in your hand and insert the other end into the water so that it just breaks the surface. Slowly rub the smooth stick over the notched one. Each time a notch is hit, a compression wave is produced. When that happens in the air, it becomes a sound wave. When the wave is produced in the water, part of the compression wave becomes a sound wave and part becomes a water wave.

Sound waves move in mediums (solids, gases, or liquids), but not in vacuums. Have you ever seen an old Western movie where the wise Indian tracker puts his ear to the ground to listen for a galloping horse or herd of buffalo? It really works. Here are two ways you can demonstrate this for yourself:

You can hear the sounds of passing traffic by placing your ear to the ground.

1. Place your ear to a tabletop and then scratch your fingernails across the tabletop. You will hear the vibrations from your fingernails coming through the tabletop.
2. Next time you find yourself at an appropriate place—such as a ball field, a farm, a sidewalk where people walk—find an out-of-the-way spot where you won't be in the way, and put your ear to the ground. If there is any movement of people, horses, cows, and so forth, you should be able to hear the vibrations they set up as they step across the ground.

Trick 2
"Break" Your Nose
EFFECT: You gently place your face down on a tabletop. Your nose should be touching it. You then

roll your head sideways from left to right. It sounds as if you broke your nose.

PROPS
    a tabletop
    a quarter

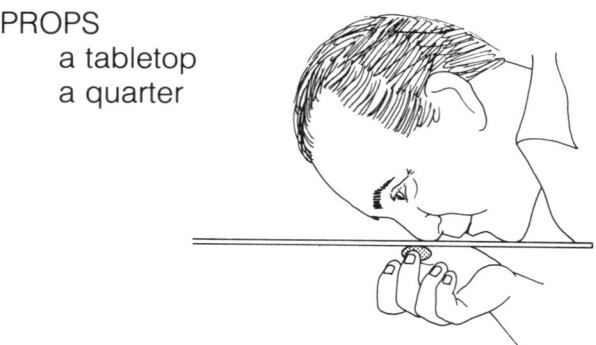

ROUTINE
Your friends are not aware that you are holding the quarter in your right fingertips. Place your right hand underneath the table with one edge of the coin touching the underside of the tabletop. Just as you start to roll your head from left to right, let the quarter snap against the underside of the tabletop. It will sound as if you broke your nose. The sound is being transmitted through the wood to the air to your friend's ears.

Betcha 4

> **THIS MAY BE DANGEROUS.
> TO BE PERFORMED ONLY WITH ADULT SUPERVISION**

Tell your friend, "I bet that I can place this buzzer inside this juice jar and muffle the sound without covering the jar with insulation like a towel or blanket."

PROPS
   a juice jar
   a small buzzer from an electronics store
   a battery to operate the buzzer
   a cork large enough to fit in the mouth of the jar
   a piece of paper—12 inches long and ½-inch wide
   matches

ROUTINE
Suspend the buzzer in the jar by its wires. The wires should extend outside of the jar. Place the cork in the bottle. Touch the battery's electrodes to the proper wires of the buzzer and listen to the intensity of the buzz. Remove the cork and the buzzer from the bottle.

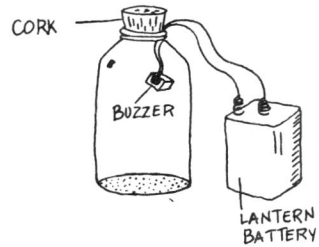

Light one end of the paper with the match and drop it into the bottle. When the fire burns itself out, wait a moment, then once again suspend the buzzer in the jar by its wires, the wires extending outside of the jar. Then place the cork in the bottle. Touch the battery's electrodes to the proper wires of the buzzer once again and listen to the intensity of the buzz. It will be muffled.

EXPLANATION: The burning slip of paper heated the air, causing it to expand and rise out of the mouth of the jar. By placing the buzzer and cork into the jar's mouth, an airtight seal is formed. As the jar cools down, the air contained within contracts. A partial vacuum is formed. Since sound needs air molecules to spread out, the sound from the jar is now less intense.

HEARING OR SOUND PERCEPTION

We hear sounds because the vibrations of the sound waves are collected by our outer ears and moved to our ear canals. The waves then hit our eardrums, causing them to vibrate. These vibrations are turned into nerve impulses that we know as sound.

Because we have two ears, we can usually tell where a sound is coming from—front, back, or sides. That's how stereos work. The sound waves come from two different speakers. The speakers are usually on opposite sides of a room, or, if you're wearing headphones, on opposite sides of your head. When music is recorded in stereo, you will hear certain instruments from one speaker and other instruments from the other speaker. Some stereo demonstration records make it sound as though a train, plane, herd of cows, or car was actually in the room with you, passing from one side of the room to the other.

We can usually tell where a sound is coming from, but we can trick our ears into believing a sound is coming from somewhere else.

Experiment 6

Stand behind a friend and ask him to raise his right hand when the sound comes from the right, the left hand when the sound comes from the left, and to tell you when the sound is in the middle. Snap your finger to his right side, left side, and directly in the middle of his back. This experiment shows how we perceive the direction sound is coming from.

Now take the cardboard inner core from a roll of paper towels, and have your friend place one end of it to his right ear. Do the experiment again, and you will find that his perception is a little different this time. The sound has to travel a longer distance to get to the ear with the tube next to it. When you snap your fingers in back of his head this time, he will be sure that the sound was coming from his left side. Experiment to find out where you have to position your finger snap to make him think it's in the middle.

This next trick will show you how difficult it is to pinpoint the exact location of sound.

Trick 3
Three Matchbox Monte
EFFECT: You have three matchboxes on the table in front of you. You pick them up one at a time and shake them. One of them rattles as though it contained a small weight, and the other two are silent. You ask your audience to guess which box has the weight inside, and they are always unable to do so.

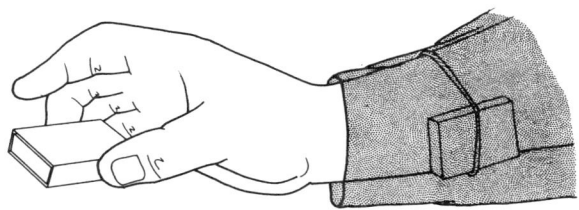

PROPS
    4 small, empty matchboxes
    a small weight like a washer or machinist's nut
    a rubber band

SETUP
Wear a long-sleeved shirt. Put the rubber band around your left wrist. Place the weight inside one matchbox. Close the matchbox and secure it to your wrist by placing it under the rubber band. Button your cuffs so no one will see the matchbox.

ROUTINE
Pick up one matchbox with your right hand and shake it. Put it back on the table. Pick up the second matchbox with your left hand and shake it. The audience will hear the rattling coming from the hidden matchbox, but will assume it to be coming from the

matchbox in view. Put the second matchbox back on the tabletop. Pick up the third matchbox with your right hand, shake it, and put it back on the tabletop.

The audience has seen you shake three matchboxes. Only one has rattled. Now ask them to find the one that rattles.

Whichever one they pick up and shake will not rattle. Show them which one is the correct one by picking up your selection with your left hand and rattling it.

EXPLANATION: The ear can pick up the general direction of a noise but not the precise location.

Trick 4
A Nasty Gag
EFFECT: When a friend bends over to pick up something from the floor, a tearing sound occurs.

PROP
   an old piece of bedsheet material

ROUTINE
This trick is to be done on the spur of the moment, when the occasion arises. If you are ever standing behind a friend and he starts to bend over, pull the cloth out of your pocket, and rip it in half. Your friend will think that his pants ripped.

NOTE: You should be standing directly behind your friend when you do this. He will not know exactly where the sound is coming from, only that it is someplace behind him. Because of that, he will think that his pants split down the seam.

CONTROLLING SOUND DISPERSAL

A little earlier in this book, we found out that sound waves spread out in the shape of a ball. If you could control the spread of the sound, you would be able to concentrate it in one direction. In the days before electronic intercoms, sailors had a method of communicating from one deck of a ship to another by taking advantage of the fact that sound could be channeled. They used speaking tubes. These were empty tubes (except for air) that stretched from one deck to another. When a sailor spoke into one end of the tube, he was heard at the other end.

You can make a speaking tube very easily.

Experiment 7
APPARATUS
   a garden hose

PROCEDURE
Stretch the garden hose out as far as you can. Hold one end and have a friend hold the other. When you talk into the tube, he should listen; when he talks, you should listen. The sound waves travel down the tube, and because they are fairly concentrated (they didn't spread out), you should be able to hear each other pretty well.

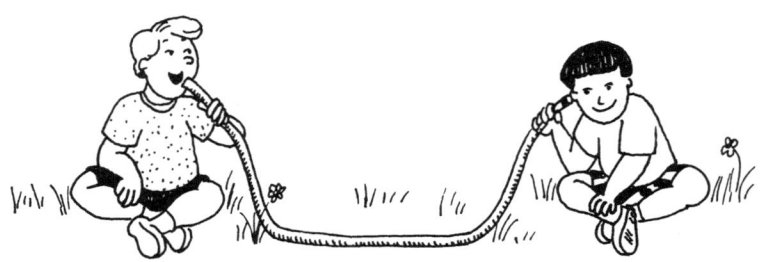

Another way to concentrate the sound waves toward a particular direction is with the use of a megaphone. Cheerleaders used megaphones years ago so their cheers would be heard. The cone of the megaphone helped to prevent the sound waves from spreading out to the sides and assisted in projecting them straight ahead.

Before electronic hearing aids, hearing-impaired people sometimes used a reverse-megaphone device called a hearing trumpet to improve their hearing. The cone helped to concentrate sound waves and guide them to the person's ear.

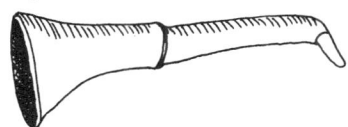

A hearing trumpet. The smaller end went into the ear; the wider end pointed in the direction of the sound.

SPEED OF SOUND

Just about every substance that you can name is to some degree elastic (having the ability to return to an original shape after being deformed or bent out of shape). It is this elasticity that allows compression waves to travel through substances. Because of the different amounts of elasticity of materials, sound travels at different speeds in different materials.

NOTE: Don't forget that sound cannot travel in a vacuum. Following is a list of the speed of sound in various materials at approximately 20° Celsius at sea level.

SPEED OF SOUND TABLE

MATERIAL	SPEED (ft/sec)	(miles/hour) (approx)
Carbon dioxide (CO_2)	877	597
Air	1,126	770
Hydrogen (H)	4,315	2,942
Water (H_2O)	4,800	3,286
Brass	11,500	7,840
Granite	12,950	8,829
Steel	16,700	11,386

    Compare the speed of sound in the different materials listed. The speed of sound is more than four times as fast in water as it is in air, and more than eleven times faster in granite than in air.

    Sound does not travel well through matter like sawdust, carpeting, foam rubber, or clay because these items are not very elastic.

How Far Away Is a Lightning Flash?

When lightning flashes, an electrical discharge occurs in the atmosphere. This force sets up compression waves in the air. The compression waves arrive at the speed of sound in air (1,126 feet/second). We know this compression wave as thunder. By calculating the length of time it takes for the thunder to reach us, we can figure out how far away the lightning has struck. (Note: The speed of light is considered instantaneous for this observation.)

How far away is a lightning flash?

First, calculate the length of time that it takes sound to go one mile in air. To do that, find out what percentage of a mile it goes in one second. Sound moves at 1,126 ft/sec and a mile is 5,280 feet, so if we divide 1,126 by 5,280, we find that it goes about 20 percent of a mile in 1 second, which means that it takes about 5 seconds to go one mile. (5 × 20 percent = 100 percent)

Next time there is a thunderstorm, watch for a lightning flash, then count the number of seconds until you hear the thunder. Divide the number of seconds by five to get the approximate distance in miles.

EXAMPLE: If you were to see a stroke of lightning in the distance, and you counted off fourteen seconds until you heard the thunder, your calculations would look like this:

$$\frac{\text{total time from seeing lightning to hearing thunder}}{5 \text{ (approximate length of time for sound to go one mile)}} = \text{distance in miles from lightning}$$

or

$$14/5 = 2\,4/5 \text{ or } 2.8 \text{ miles}$$

NOTE: You can see and hear the difference in the speed of sound and the speed of light at a big-league ball park. The next time you're at a game, watch and listen carefully when a great hitter like Darryl Strawberry or Bo Jackson comes to bat. See when he hits the ball, then listen for the crack of the bat. You will observe that the sound arrives sometime after the actual hit.

BREAKING THE SOUND BARRIER

When people talk of breaking the sound barrier, they mean "going faster than the speed of sound." At ground level, that means going faster than 770 miles per hour (mph). At higher levels in the atmosphere, the speed of sound drops to well under 700 mph. When a jet travels faster than the speed of sound, and you observe it from outside the plane, you will see the plane in one place and hear the roar of its engines somewhere behind it. When an object breaks the sound barrier, it creates a sonic boom, which sounds like an explosion. As the plane passes through the sound barrier, it makes a tremendous amount of vibrations. These vibrations are the direct cause of the boom.

If you are in a plane that is breaking the sound barrier, you will not hear the boom because you are moving faster than sound. You are actually outrunning the sound at that point. Anyone outside of the plane will be affected by the noise.

A sonic boom is a frightfully loud noise that also sets up dangerous vibrations in solid objects that can lead to their destruction. The supersonic transport (SST) that travels between Europe and the United States does not travel at supersonic speeds (faster than sound) over populated areas because

of these destructive waves. These waves have been known to break solid objects such as window glass. If strong enough, they can cause walls to vibrate so violently that they fall down.

The first object made by humans to break the sound barrier was invented centuries ago. It's the whip. Many people think that a whip makes a noise when it's cracked because the tip hits the ground. Those folks are wrong. The whip is used in such a

fashion that the tip (cracker) on the end breaks the sound barrier. When that happens, a sonic boom occurs, and that is the noise that you hear. That's also the reason why whips are so dangerous. Even though the tip of the whip is lightweight and has comparatively little mass, it is moving so rapidly that when it hits something, it releases a tremendous amount of kinetic energy over a small concentrated area.

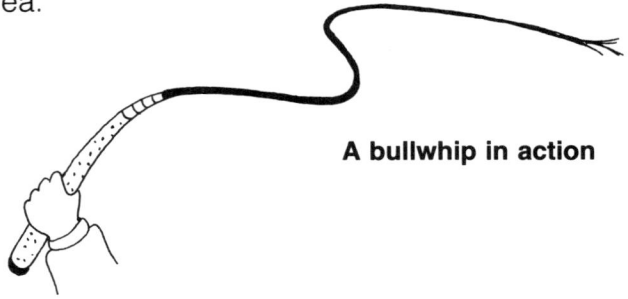

A bullwhip in action

EFFECT OF TEMPERATURE ON SOUND

The speed of sound in solids and liquids is barely affected by temperature. Its effect is so small that we can practically ignore it. When sound travels through a gas, however, the temperature of the gas has a definite influence on its speed. Sound moves faster through a hot gas than a cool gas. The molecules of a hot gas are moving more rapidly than the molecules of a cooler gas.

When relatively small changes in temperature occur, such as everyday temperature swings on Earth, there is a change of about 2 ft/sec for every degree Celsius. Sound moves faster in warmer air, slower in cooler air. Sound travels at 1,126 ft/sec at

20° Celsius (68°F). At 10°C (50°F), sound will travel at 1,086 ft/sec.

(10 degrees difference)
1,126 − 10 × 2 = 1,086

You can hear the difference in the speed of sound at varying temperatures at a large field or other grassy area. On a hot summer day, the distance that noise travels over the ground is fairly short. The air near the ground is warmer than the air above it. Remember, sound travels faster in warmer air than in cooler air. The waves get bent in an upward direction when they reach the cooler air and travel away from the ground.

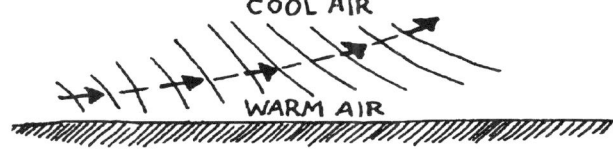

On a summer night that is cooler than the day just gone by, the opposite happens. The air near the ground is cooler than the air above. When the sound waves start to move from the cooler air to the warmer air, they get bent into a downward direction, toward the ground, and will travel farther than they would during the heat of the day.

ECHOES

Echoes are caused by the reflection of sound waves from distant objects. This sound reflection is similar to reflections you see in a mirror. Sound waves go out, hit an object, and are reflected back. When lightning "strikes" and makes its noise, the sound waves are often reflected back and forth between the ground and the clouds, making a "rolling thunder" sound. Some sound reflectors are better than others. The best reflectors are hard things like stone, brick, or concrete walls. The poorest reflectors are soft things like foam rubber, carpeting, and drapes.

Experiment 8
APPARATUS
   a 20-foot length of clothesline

PROCEDURE
Tie the rope to a door handle. Extend the free end of the rope as far as you can and hold it tightly. Make sure that the area in which you are doing this is clear, with no obstructions. Give your end of the rope a sudden up-and-down snap. You will see a "wave" travel down the rope, hit the other end, and travel back to your hand. If you hold the rope taut, the

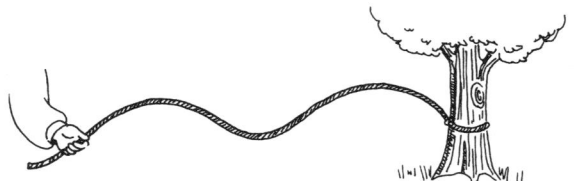

You may tie the rope to a tree instead of a door handle.

wave will probably travel back and forth a few times before it dies out.

An echo is a reflection of sound waves. As the sound wave is reflected in this experiment, a sound wave is reflected through the air to cause an echo. In order for us to hear two different sounds, they must occur at least 1/10–1/15 seconds apart. If they hit the ear closer together in time, they are heard as one sound, not two. That means that for us to hear an echo, the original sound and reflected sound must be separated by at least 1/10–1/15 seconds.

In order for us to hear an echo of our own voice, or any other noise that we make, we must be at least 56 feet from a reflecting surface, because sound travels 1,126 feet in one second. In 1/10 of a second, sound travels about 112 feet. If we are 56 feet from the sound-reflecting wall, it will take 1/20 of a second for a sound we make to reach the wall and another 1/20 of a second for the sound to come back to us. Since $1/20 + 1/20 = 1/10$, we must be at least 56 feet from the wall to hear an echo.

Experiment 9
APPARATUS
    2 solid blocks of wood
    a measuring tape
    a stopwatch

NOTE: You will need a friend to help with this experiment.

PROCEDURE
Find a building with a solid wall that is at least 100 feet from the street. Start at the wall and knock the blocks together, hard enough to cause a sharp noise. (Make sure that you don't have your fingers in between the blocks, or you'll really hate this experiment.) Listen for an echo. Move straight away from

Timing an echo

the wall, at approximately 10-foot intervals. Each time you have reached a 10-foot mark, knock the blocks together again, all the time listening for an echo. When you finally hear an echo, mark that spot on the ground and measure the distance to the wall. You will find that the distance is between 37 and 56 feet away from the wall.

From that point on, have a friend try to measure the length of time from when the noise is first heard to the time that the echo is heard, increasing the distance with each test. If your friend has an accurate timing finger, you will find that you can measure your distance to the wall by calculating the distance that the sound travels in the time that is measured.

SONAR

Sonar (*so*und *na*vigation *r*anging), used by the navies of the world to detect submarines, works on the same general principle that you used in Experiment 9. Here's a simplified version of how sonar works. The searching ship sends out a "ping" of sound. When that "ping" hits a submarine, the sound is

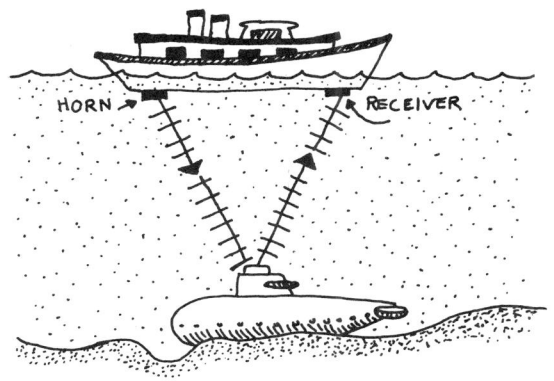

reflected back to the sending ship, and the sonar unit computes the distance between. It calculates the distance by multiplying the speed of sound in water and the amount of time that it takes for the reflected "ping" to return, divided by two.

CONTINUOUS WAVES

Once vibrations stop, sound stops. Once again, that's why you can't hear sounds in a vacuum. Sound vibrations are carried by matter. No matter, no sound.

When you listen to your stereo, the speakers are constantly vibrating, causing sound. When you listen to a CD or tape, the stereo turns the information on the disc or tape into electrical impulses that vibrate the speakers. The speakers set up compression waves in the air that we hear as music. As long as continuous waves are being produced by the speakers, we hear sound. The moment these continuous waves stop, we hear nothing. This happens in between tunes or when a disc or tape has finished playing.

Experiment 10

Tape a piece of paper to each speaker of your stereo as shown in the illustration. Turn the music on to a very soft setting and look at the papers. Increase the volume and again look at the papers. The higher (louder) the volume, the more the papers flutter about. The speakers are moving back and forth, creating sound waves.

Remove the cloth grill (if it is removable) in front of the speaker. If the cloth is nonremovable, don't do this part of the experiment. Once the speaker diaphragm is visible, play a CD or tape. Observe how the speaker moves. At times you will see it move rapidly, at other times slowly. Sometimes it will move great distances, other times, small distances. These movements are vibrations that set up the compression waves that you know as music.

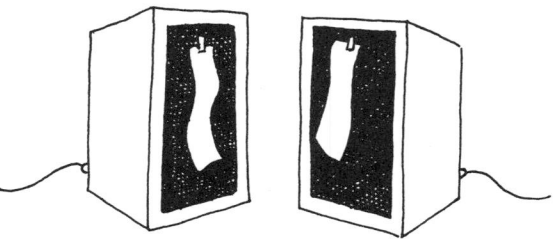

CAUTION: Do not touch the inside of the speaker. This is usually quite delicate and easily damaged.

WAVELENGTH AND FREQUENCY

Sound is affected by both wavelength and wave frequency. Frequency is the number of waves per second or number of vibrations per second (how many vibrations move past a given point in one second).

A wavelength is the distance between two points that are in the same consecutive position in a complete wave. The wave may be measured from crest to crest (high point to high point), trough to trough (low point to low point), or from any other set

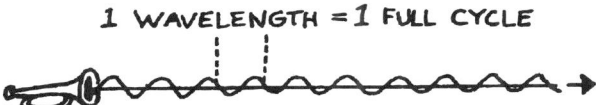

of points that you wish to use. No matter what points are chosen, as long as they are at the same height in the wave train, and are in the same state of compression or relaxation (going up or coming down), the wavelength will always be the same. The points where you measure the wavelength don't matter.

One complete wavelength is called a cycle. Frequency is sometimes measured in cycles per second (the number of cycles that pass a particular point in a second).

ACOUSTICS

The dictionary defines acoustics as: 1) the science that deals with sound; 2) the qualities in a room that make it easy or hard for a person to hear distinctly. Sound waves are usually present all around us. We can't escape from sounds.

Experiment 11
Go into the quietest room in your house, when you're all alone, and lie down on the floor. Don't move. Listen as hard as you can. What do you hear?

You might hear a little noise from outside the house, maybe traffic, or people talking or a plane flying overhead. Try to cut that noise out by covering your ears with a towel or a blanket. (Make sure that you can breathe.) What do you hear now?

You might hear a little rustling of your hair or body against the towel, or you might hear yourself breathing. Hold your breath, lie as still as possible, and listen carefully. What do you hear now?

Even if you hold your breath perfectly, you'll probably hear your heart beating or your stomach talking. It's practically impossible to cut yourself off from all sounds.

There are many sounds that we wish to hear such as someone talking, a movie, a TV show, music, a doorbell that means your best friend has come over to visit.

There are sounds that we usually don't want to hear. We call these sounds noise! Is there something that can turn a sound we like into noise? Why does sound behave in different ways in different places? Is there a science to music?

To a musician, "pitch" is the highness or lowness of a sound, or where it falls on a musical scale. The pitch is generally the frequency of a sound. The higher the frequency (the faster the sounds move past a point), the higher the pitch. In music, a "tone" is perceived only when the vibrations (sound waves) have a specific frequency. If the vibrations are uneven, the sound is called noise.

Experiment 12
APPARATUS
    a playing card
    a clothespin
    a bicycle

PREPARATION
Attach the card to the fork of your bicycle with the clothespin, so that it will hit the spokes of the wheel.

PROCEDURE
Start to pedal your bike down the block at a steady, even pace. You will hear the "ratatatatatat" of the card hitting the spokes. Now pedal a little faster, and you will hear the sound go up in pitch. When you pedal faster, the card hits the spokes at a quicker rate. The frequency of the "ratatatats" has increased. Remember: pitch is increased by increasing the frequency.

Note the card attached on fork with clothespin.

Trick 5
The Messed-up Answering Machine
EFFECT: You call up a friend who has an answering machine and leave a message. All of a sudden, it will sound to your friend as though his answering machine is messed up.

PROPS
  a two-speed micro-cassette tape recorder

METHOD

Before leaving the message on your friend's machine, record your message on the micro-cassette. Tape half the message at the high speed, then flick the speed change switch, and record the rest of the message at the low speed. When you play back the message, do it at high speed only. Your message will sound normal at first and then sound very high pitched and distorted, almost like a cartoon voice. Now call up your friend's machine, and play the recording, instead of talking yourself. Your friend will think that his answering machine is acting nutty.

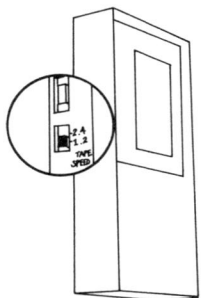

NOTE: Your voice sounds strange when played at a higher speed because the pitch has changed. My recorder has two speeds: 1.2 (inches of tape moving past the recording/playback head per second) and 2.4 (inches of tape moving past the recording/playback head per second). That means that there are twice the vibrations per second, and a voice on a speeded-up portion of tape will sound darned funny.

SILENT SOUNDS

There are sound waves that cannot be heard by humans. The average human can hear sounds with frequencies from approximately 20 to 20,000 cycles (full vibrations or complete waves) per second. Sound that has a frequency lower than 20 cycles is called *subsonic*. Even though we can't hear these sounds with our ears, we can sometimes sense them. Subsonics have been known to cause structures to start vibrating and have also caused feelings of illness in humans. Spies would sometimes use subsonics to make enemy agents feel ill.

Sounds that are above 20,000 cycles are called *ultrasonic*. Some animals can detect sounds at levels above our range of hearing. Dogs have often been trained to respond to silent (to us) whistles. Ultrasonic waves that move at the rate of over 100,000 cycles are used for many things in everyday life. Machinery based on ultrasonic technology kills bacteria, cleans jewelry and other metallic items, and helps purify the air around us.

THE DOPPLER EFFECT

When a train with its whistle blasting approaches you at a high rate of speed, the pitch of the whistle seems to slowly get higher the closer it gets, but once it passes, the pitch rapidly decreases. We said that pitch is the frequency of sound waves—how many vibrations hit our ears per second. As the train approaches, the sound waves arrive at an increasing rate. The distance between you and the whistle is decreasing at a rapid speed. This causes an increase in the pitch because more waves are striking your ear per second than if both you and the train were standing still. When the train passes you by, the sound waves of the whistle reach your ears at a decreasing rate, lowering the pitch, because less waves per second are reaching your ears.

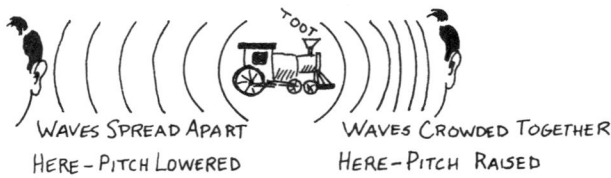

WAVES SPREAD APART
HERE - PITCH LOWERED

WAVES CROWDED TOGETHER
HERE - PITCH RAISED

LOUDNESS

You know what wavelength and frequency are. The next measurement of sound is the *amplitude*. When we measured wavelength, we went from crest to crest or trough to trough. Frequency is the number of waves passing a given point in one second. The amplitude is the height from the bottom of a trough to the top of a crest.

Sound studios and laboratories use an instrument called an *oscilloscope*. The oscilloscope can change sound waves, collected by a microphone, into visible waves on a TV-type screen. If you had access to an oscilloscope, you would actually be able to compare different wavelengths. If you could produce just one frequency of sound, maybe by gently blowing one note on a harmonica, you would see a wave of a certain amplitude on the screen. If you blew that same note again, but did it more forcefully so it was louder, you would find that the wavelength remains the same, but the amplitude increases. The higher the amplitude, the louder the sound. The lower the amplitude, the softer the sound. We call this loudness or softness the *intensity* of a sound. The greater the amplitude, the greater the intensity. The amplitude of the sound wave is one of two things that determines how intense or loud a sound really is. The other ingredient of loudness is the distance of the ear from the sound generator. Under perfect conditions (no wind and no echoes), a sound will generally fall off inversely as the square of the distance.

To do this calculation, you make a fraction of the distance, with one as the numerator, and the distance itself as the denominator. Multiply that fraction by itself.

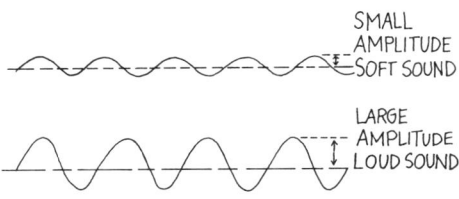

distance	inverse	×	itself	intensity at distance
2 feet	½	×	½	¼
3 feet	⅓	×	⅓	1/9
4 feet	¼	×	¼	1/16
5 feet	⅕	×	⅕	1/25
6 feet	⅙	×	⅙	1/36

This means that at a distance of five feet, the sound is only 1/25th as loud as at one foot. At a distance of 500 feet, the sound is only 1/25th as loud as at 100 feet.

The intensity of the sound when it is received is measured in *decibels* (db). A whisper is about 20 db, everyday talking is about 50 to 60 db, noisy machinery about 90 to 100 db. Some live music

Rustling leaves and whispers cause low intensity sounds.

concerts generate intensity readings of over 120 db, which is also the threshold of pain.

Some rock bands cause high intensity sounds.

If you are subjected to 100 db of sound or greater for a short length of time, you can feel pain and a partial, temporary hearing loss. If subjected to sound intensities of 100 db or higher for extended periods, permanent hearing loss may occur.

Decibel Levels of Some Common Sounds

rustling leaves	5 db
whisper	15 db
car noise—running on highway	45 db
everyday talking	55 db
street traffic	75 db
subway noise	100 db
thunder	110 db
loud music concert	125+ db

SOUND QUALITY

Pure tones of only a single, simple wave are rarely produced. The notes that we hear are usually the fundamental, along with several harmonics. That is why even though the same note may be played on two different musical instruments such as a piano and a clarinet, they will sound different. The fundamentals may be identical, but there are many intricate harmonics being added to the original sound.

INDOOR ACOUSTICS

One of the definitions of acoustics is "the qualities in a room that make it easy or hard for a person to hear distinctly."

First, we have to compare indoor sounds to outdoor. When we listen to music or conversation in the open air, we notice a few things:

- The sound intensity (loudness) fades quickly with distance.
- Wind, breezes, and other weather conditions affect the sound, usually in an unfavorable way.
- The sound that we hear seems a little stale or dead.
- Uncontrollable echoes sometimes make it difficult to hear well.

Examples can be heard at a baseball game. The announcements from the public address system are usually hard to understand for any one, or possibly a combination, of the above reasons.

When we listen to music or conversation indoors, we run into different factors that affect sounds, but these can be controlled to some de-

gree. When we're indoors in a theater, the sound waves reflect from walls, the ceiling, and other surfaces with the result that the sound intensity is generally uniform throughout. A well-designed theater will add "life" to the sound, by allowing the sound waves to reach a listener at slightly different times (less than 1/10 of a second). This minute difference in time adds a richness to the sound that would not ordinarily exist out of doors.

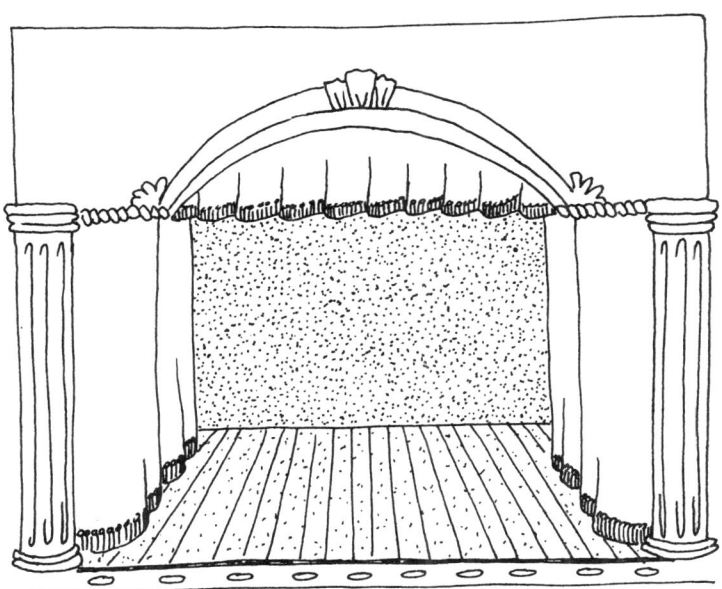

A poorly designed room may have surfaces that are too hard and reflect the sound back and forth a number of times. These hard surfaces can be modified by hanging drapery or sound-deadening material in front of them. If these hard reflecting surfaces are not covered, musical notes or spoken words will be combined with the echoes, causing much confusion.

STANDING WAVES

Waves can pass right through each other without affecting each other.

Experiment 13
Fill your bathtub or kitchen sink with water. Fill two glasses with water. Slowly spill some water into one corner of the sink. Look at the ripples that are set

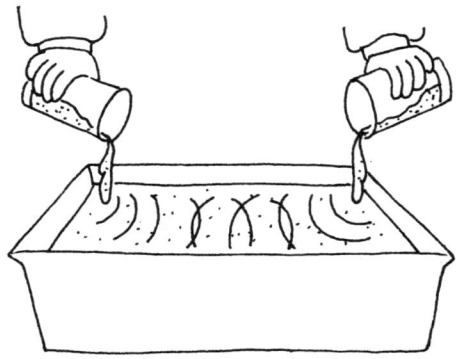

up. See how they spread in an ever-widening circle. Slowly spill some water into the diagonally opposite corner. Examine those ripples. Now, with the two glasses, set up ripples in both corners. Examine the ripples and notice how they pass right through each other.

Sound waves work the same way. Have you ever noticed how you can listen to a music tape and hear individual singers and instruments? If the sound waves interfered with each other, we wouldn't be able to tell the difference between the singer, the guitar, drums, or piano. It would all sound like noise. We can also talk to friends while we listen to music.

In Experiment 8, you used a 20-foot length of heavy rope to make a mechanical model of wave reflection. Using the same clothesline, you can investigate standing waves (stationary waves).

Experiment 14

Tie the rope to a door handle that is at least three feet above the ground. Extend the free end of the rope as far as you can and hold it tightly. Make sure that the area in which you are doing this is clear, with no obstructions. In Experiment 8, you just gave the rope a sudden up-and-down snap. The result, if you remember, was a "wave" traveling down the rope, hitting the other end, and traveling back to your hand. This time, instead of one up-and-down snap, try to waggle the rope up and down in a regular, repeated manner.

There will be two consistent, continual waves traveling up and down the rope. The first is the wave going down the rope, the second is the wave coming back (the reflected wave).

The two ends of the rope, the one you're holding and the one tied to the doorknob, are stationary (not moving). Using trial and error, you will be able to find a rate where it seems there are no waves moving back and forth. The rope will simply look like an arch or loop that is moving up, then down. The wave motion will seem to disappear.

Have a friend time the number of up-and-down motions of the hand shaking the rope for 5 seconds. Multiply that number by 12 and you will have the frequency per minute. Double that frequency and another balanced pattern appears. The rope will have two steady arches, or loops. The middle point of the rope will not move, as though it were held in place by something. These are called standing waves. The point where the rope remains stationary is called a *node*.

NOTE: Achieving these effects will take some practice.

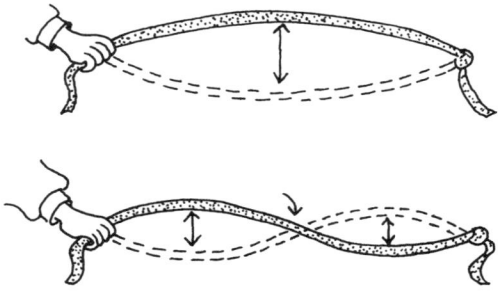

STRINGED INSTRUMENTS

The strings of musical instruments, such as violins, banjos, and guitars, move in exactly the same way

as the rope in Experiment 14. When the instrument's string is set in motion, it will vibrate with one loop, and the sound we hear will be the lowest possible note from that string. That note is called the *fundamental*.

If you touch the string in the middle and then pluck it, it will vibrate with two loops. The two-loop note is called the *first harmonic*. Because the first harmonic has two waves instead of one, it is twice the frequency of the first loop. You can set up three, four, or five waves in a string by touching it at different points.

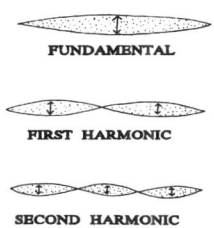

FUNDAMENTAL

FIRST HARMONIC

SECOND HARMONIC

Experiment 15
APPARATUS
  a cake pan
  a dowel or other stick
  a few rubber bands (some thick, some thin)

PREPARATION
Use any rubber band and look at the illustration.

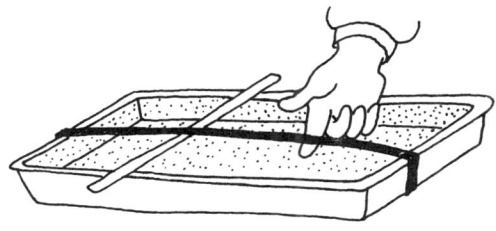

PROCEDURE
1. With one rubber band in place, pluck it and listen to the sound. Place the dowel under the center of the rubber band. Pluck the rubber band in the center of one side and listen to the resultant sound. This is the first harmonic. Experiment on your own by moving the dowel one-third of the way from the right end of the cake pan, and striking the left-hand side of the string. That will give you the third harmonic.

   When you shorten the string, you raise the pitch. That's what happens when you see guitarists, banjoists, or violinists moving their fingers up and down the neck of their instruments. They're changing the lengths of the strings, and thereby changing the harmonics.
2. Select a rubber band of a different thickness. Place it one inch away from the rubber band already on the cake pan. Try to get the same amount of tension on each one. Pluck them. Notice how the heavier rubber band will sound lower in pitch.

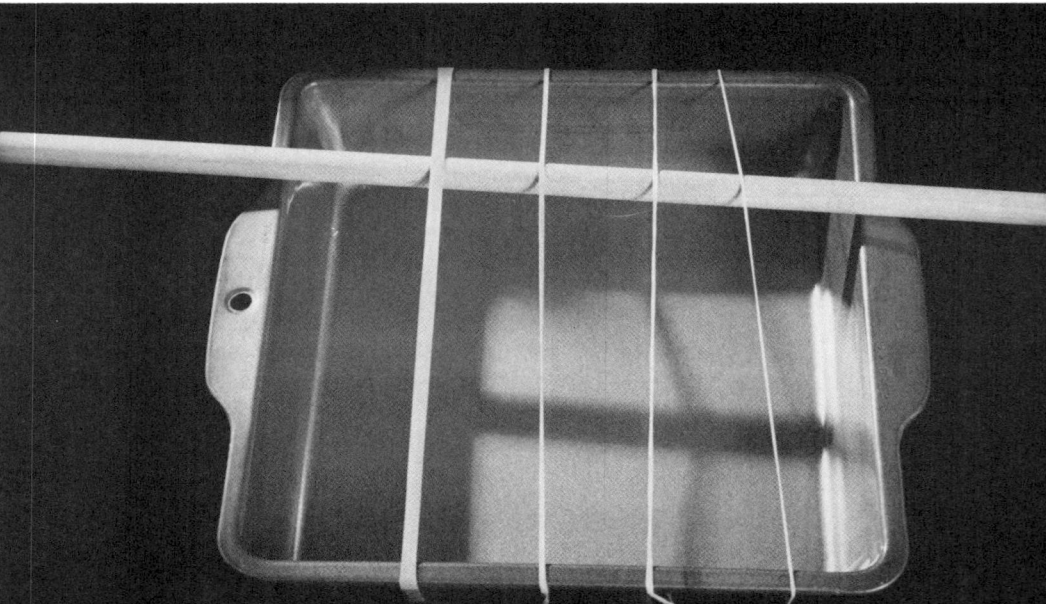

3. Select two rubber bands of the same thickness. Place them one inch away from each other on the cake pan. Adjust them so that one is tighter than the other. Pluck each of them. Notice how the tighter one has a higher pitch.

This experiment has shown that the pitch can be altered on a string by shortening it, by changing the tension on it, or by changing the thickness of it.

It is important for a player of a stringed instrument to know how to change the pitch by using these different methods. If the musician doesn't know them, you can be sure that the music will sound less than wonderful.

WIND INSTRUMENTS

Instruments that produce notes by wind, such as the pipe organ, clarinet, saxophone, or flute, are like the stringed instruments in at least one respect. Standing waves are set up by these instruments. These waves, however, are in columns of air rather than in

strings. Instead of crests and troughs along a string, we have the compression and expansion of air.

There are two possibilities:

1. If you blow into a pipe, a compression wave starts at the end you blow into and travels to the other end at the speed of sound. If the pipe is blocked off at that other end, the wave reflects back and comes out the end where it started. If you keep up a steady blowing from your end, this traveling back and forth is steady. The frequency or pitch is determined by the length of the tube.

What we have just described is a pipe organ like the ones found in many churches. Each pipe in an organ can produce only one specific note.

Experiment 16
APPARATUS
    a kitchen sink
    a large glass bottle, such as a one-gallon apple juice jug

PROCEDURE
Place the jug on the bottom of the sink with the mouth

of the jug positioned directly under the water spigot. Start to fill the jug with water, and listen to the changing sound as the jug gets fuller. As the water fills up the jug, the length of the "tube" (the empty space in the jug) gets smaller and smaller, and the pitch gets higher and higher.

2. If the end of the pipe is open, the wave is not reflected, but keeps on traveling out the other end. The length of the pipe still determines the frequency.

Experiment 17

APPARATUS
 a plastic soda straw
 scissors

PROCEDURE

Trim one end of the straw, as shown in the illustration. Place the trimmed end of the straw between your lips and blow into it with a "ptptptptptptptpt" sound, by vibrating your lips as you exhale. While you're "ptptptptptptping," cut little pieces of straw from the other end of the straw. Listen to the sound as you cut. The pitch gets higher and higher. The pitch is determined by the length of the pipe. The shorter the pipe, the higher the pitch.

This is how instruments such as the pennywhistle, saxophone, trumpet, clarinet, and oboe produce music. These instruments can produce a variety of notes because they have openings along the side of the pipe that may be opened or closed, effectively changing the length of the tube and the length of the wave. A trombone changes the pitch by changing the length of the pipe.

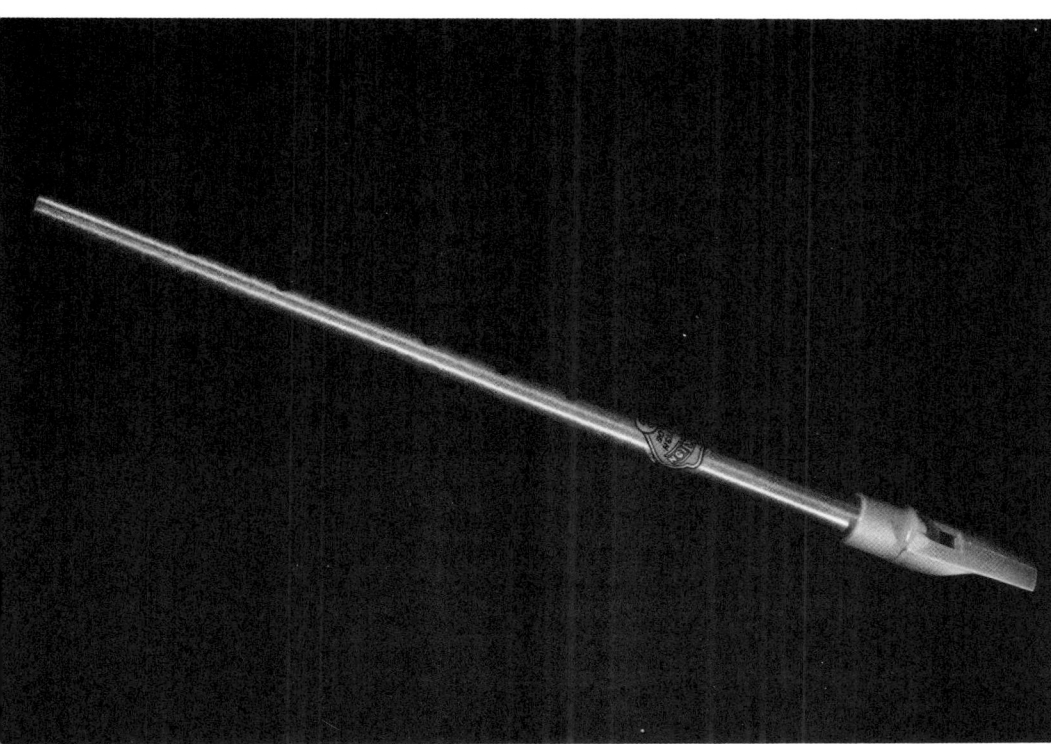

When the music box is held underneath the empty wooden box, the wooden box acts as a soundboard.

RESONANCE

Resonance is the addition of waves to each other.

Experiment 18
APPARATUS
   a large, empty can
   a piece of wire coat hanger
   strong string
   a very weak magnet
   hammer
   nail
   sand
   epoxy glue

PREPARATION
Punch two holes in the rim of the empty can with the hammer and nail. The holes should be at the very top and opposite each other. Put the piece of wire hanger through both holes. Bend each end of the wire so it won't fall out of the can. Tie the string to the center of the wire. Attach the string to the overhead center of a doorway. (Get your parent's permission and help to drive a small nail into the doorframe.) Fill the can with sand. Glue a piece of string to one side of the magnet.

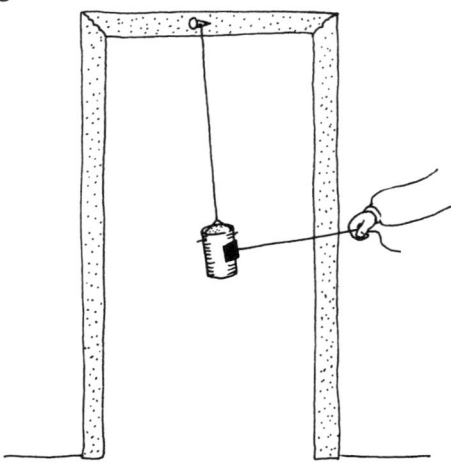

PROCEDURE
Put the magnet on the side of the can. It should stick by magnetic attraction. Try to pull the can toward you with the magnet. If the magnet is sufficiently weak, you won't be able to move the can very far without the magnet falling off. Attach the magnet a second time. Slowly pull the can toward you a little bit, then relax your pull. The can will swing back the other way. When the can starts to move back to you, pull it a little bit more with the magnet, and relax again. Do this a number of times, and the weak magnet that could barely move the can before has now moved the can a great deal.

EXPLANATION: You are using a resonance to move the can. You are adding a bit of energy to each swinging motion each time it comes towards you. In acoustics, resonance can be heard when a loud noise outside your house rattles the windows. The noise may be a plane flying overhead or a truck, bus, or train going by outside. If the natural frequency of the windows is the same as noise from outside, they will start to move with *sympathetic vibrations*. (Betcha 5 will explain sympathetic vibration.)

Betcha 5

EFFECT: "I betcha that I can place a straightened-out paper clip on top of a glass and make it move around without touching it or blowing on it."

PROPS
    2 identical water glasses
    a straightened-out paper clip
    a spoon
    water

ROUTINE
Fill the two glasses with identical amounts of water. Place the paper clip so it spans the mouth of one glass. Now challenge your friend to make it move. When he admits that he is unable to do it, move the glasses close together, without letting them touch. Smack the top of the second glass lightly with the spoon. (Don't do it so hard that you'll break the

glass.) If the glasses are identical and have the same amount of water in them, they will be in resonance (vibrate at the same frequency). The second glass will start to move with sympathetic vibrations, which will cause the paper clip to move.

FORCED VIBRATIONS

A vibrating body can transfer its movement to another body. This is done frequently in musical instruments to get a louder sound from the instrument. The vibrating string will transfer its energy to a soundboard, which has a large surface area and

can put a great deal of air into motion. The more air in motion, the louder the sound. All stringed instruments, including guitars, violins, and pianos, are equipped with soundboards.

Trick 6
The Empty Music Box

EFFECT: You display a little wooden box to your friends. They hear music coming from inside it. You give the box to them to examine. They open it and find it empty.

PROPS

    a small wooden box with a hinged lid
    a small music box mechanism inside a small plastic case (usually found in novelty shops)
    a length of elastic
    safety pin

SETUP

Attach the music box to a length of elastic. The other end of the elastic is tied to a safety pin. Hook the elastic to the back of your jacket, as shown in the drawing. Before you start, wind up the music box mechanism a little bit.

ROUTINE

Hold the music box under the wooden box—they should be touching each other—and let it play. The box will pick up the vibrations and amplify them, making it seem as though the sound is coming from the wooden box. When the mechanism runs down, let it slip out from under the box and be pulled under your jacket by the elastic. At that point you may hand out the box for examination.

EXPLANATION: You have used the principle of forced vibrations to make it seem as though the music were coming from the box itself.

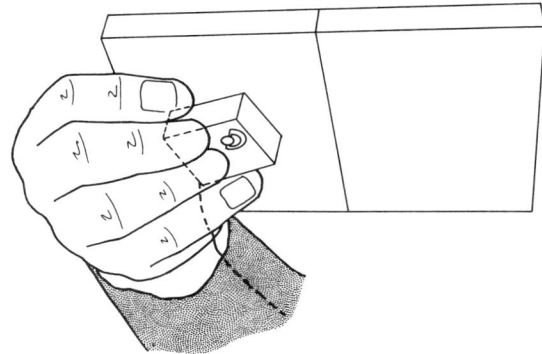

A pennywhistle's pitch changes as you cover and uncover the openings.

Trick 7
The Sound Master

EFFECT: While sitting at a table, you borrow a tuning fork. If no one has a tuning fork, a regular fork will work, if the room is very quiet. You tweak the tines of the fork to get them vibrating, then reach out and grab the "sound" from the end of the fork, and toss it into a nearby cup. Everyone will hear the sound coming from the cup.

PROPS
    a table
    a tuning fork (or regular fork, if necessary)

ROUTINE
The tabletop should be wooden, metal, or plastic and should not be covered with a tablecloth or placemats. Hold the fork as shown in the illustration. When you "tweak" the tines to get them vibrating,

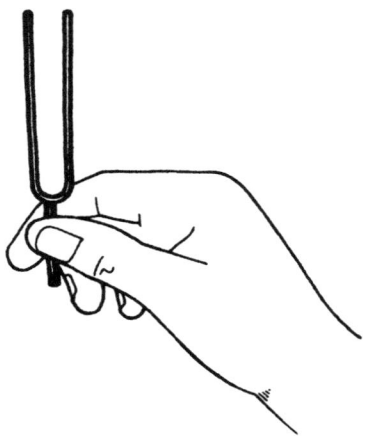

The proper way to hold the tuning fork

reach over with your free hand and make believe that you grab the sound. Don't touch the vibrating end with your hand. When you "toss the sound" into the cup, you sneakily let the thick end of the fork touch the table. The vibrations of the fork will set up forced vibrations in the tabletop. The tabletop has become a sounding board. When you draw the audience's attention to the cup, they will imagine they hear the sound coming from it.

SUPPLIERS

When asking for any of these catalogs, please mention that you saw the company's name in one of Bob Friedhoffer's books.

Johnson Smith Co.
P.O. Box 25500
Bradenton, Florida 34206-5500

Free catalog from one of the original novelty supply companies in the country

Edmund Scientific
101 E. Gloucester Pike
Barrington, New Jersey 08007-1380

Free catalog full of good things for the budding scientist

Morris & Lee Inc.
85 Botsford Place
Buffalo, New York 14216

Send for free catalog of genuine scientific apparatus at great prices

AIN Plastics
300 Park Avenue South
New York, New York 10010

Source for plastic "crystal balls" and fiberoptic rods; drop them a note to ask them about cost and availability

Mickey Hades International
Box 1414
Calgary, Alberta
Canada T2P 2L6

Send for free price list of great selection of magic books from the largest magical publisher

Paul Diamond's Mail Order Magic
P.O. Box 11570
Fort Lauderdale, Florida 33339

Good prices, good tricks, price list—$1.50; mail order only

Zanadu
772 Newark Avenue
Jersey City, New Jersey 07306

$.50 for catalog of exclusive magic effects; mail order only

Louis Tannen Inc.
6 West 32nd St.
New York, New York 10001-3808

Ask to be placed on the free mailing list of one of America's largest magic stores; visit when you're in New York

Hank Lee's Magic Factory
125 Lincoln St.
Boston, Massachusetts 02205

Ask to be placed on the free mailing list of one of America's finest and largest magic stores; visit when you're in Boston

Abbot's Magic Co.
Colon, Michigan 49040

Ask the cost of the huge catalog filled with goodies

Land of Magic
450 N.E. 20th Street
Boca Raton, Florida 33431

A great retail magic and novelty store; free mail order catalog for the asking

FOR FURTHER READING

Asimov, Isaac. *Asimov's Chronology of Science and Discovery*. New York: Harper & Row, 1989.

Bobo, J. B. *Coin Magic*. New York: Dover Publications, 1982.

Epstein, Lewis Carroll. *Thinking Physics*. San Francisco: Insight Press, 1979–1988.

Gardner, Martin. *Encyclopedia of Impromptu Magic*. Chicago: Magic Inc., 1978.

Gardner, Robert. *Famous Experiments You Can Do*. New York: Franklin Watts, 1990.

Gonick, Larry. *The Cartoon Guide to Physics*. New York: Harper Perennial, 1991.

Macauly, David. *The Way Things Work*. Boston: Houghton-Mifflin, 1988.

Tarbell, Harlan. *Tarbell Course in Magic, Vols. 1-7*. New York: Louis Tannen.

Walker, Jearl. *The Flying Circus of Physics*. New York: Wiley and Sons, 1977.

INDEX

Acoustics
   defined, 59
   experiments with, 60–62
   indoor, 68–70
Amplitude of sound, 64–67
Answering machines, experiments with, 61–62

Batteries, experiments with, 38–40
"Break" Your Nose trick, 37–38
Breaking sound barrier, 50–52
Bullwhips, 52
Buzzers, experiments with, 38–40

Cardboard tubes, experiments with, 27–28
Clotheslines, experiments with, 54–55, 71–72
Compression waves, 24–25, 32, 34, 35, 36, 48, 57
Concentrating sound waves, 47
Continuous waves, 57–58
Cups, experiments with, 32–35
Curie, Madame Marie Sklodowska, 15
Cycles (wavelengths), 59, 62–63

Decibels (db), 66–67
Diary, keeping of, 15

◆ 91 ◆

Direction of sound, experiments with, 42–44
Doppler effect, 64
Drums, 35

Eardrums, 41
Echoes, experiments with, 54–56
Einstein, Albert, 15, 17
Empty Music Box trick, 84
English measurement system, 20

Fireworks, 31, 32
First harmonic notes, 73
Forced vibrations, 83–86
Franklin, Rosalind Elsie, 15
Frequency of sound waves, 58–59
Fundamental notes, 73

Galileo Galilei, 15
Garden hoses, experiments with, 46
Gases, movement of sound in, 37, 52–53

Harmonics, 68, 73
Hearing
    defined, 32, 41
    experiments with, 32–34, 42–44

Hearing trumpets, 47
Heartbeat, 25
Hoses (garden), experiments with, 46

Indoor acoustics, 68–70
Instruments (musical)
    stringed, 72–75, 83
    wind, 75–79

Jackson, Bo, 50
Jugs, experiments with, 76–77

Light, speed of, 50
Lightning, 48–49
Liquids, movement of sound in, 37, 52
Longitudinal waves, defined, 29, 31
Loudness of sound, 64–67

Matchbook Monte trick, 43–44
Measurement systems, 20
Megaphones, 47
Messed-up Answering Machine trick, 61–62
Metric measurement system, 20
Music boxes, 79, 84
Musical instruments
    stringed, 72–75, 83
    wind, 75–79

Nasty Gag trick, 44
Noise, 60
Nose ("Break" Your) trick, 37–38
Notched sticks, experiments with, 36–37
Notebook, keeping of, 15

Oscilloscopes, 65

Paper clips, experiments with, 82–83
Paper cups, experiments with, 32–35
Pennywhistles, experiments with, 85
Physics, defined, 19
Pitch, 60, 61
Playing cards, experiments with, 60–61
Pulse, defined, 25

Reading list, 90
Reflection of sound, 54–56
Resonance
　defined, 80
　experiments with, 81–83
Rubber bands, experiments with, 73–75

Rulers, experiments with, 23–24

Silent sounds, 62–63
Solids, movement of sound in, 37, 52
Sonar, 56–57
Sonic boom, 50, 52
Sound
　amplitude of, 64–67
　controlling dispersal of, 45–47
　decibels of, 66–67
　defined, 21–22
　determining direction of, 42
　effect of temperature on, 52–53
　quality, 68
　speed of, 47–50
　vibration experiments, 23–28
Sound barrier, breaking, 50–52
Sound navigation ranging (sonar), 56–57
Sound perception. *See* Hearing
Sound reflectors (echoes), 54–56

◆ 93 ◆

Sound waves. *See*
  Waves (sound)
Soundboards, 79, 83
Sounds, silent, 62–63
Speaking tubes, 45
Speed of light, 50
Speed of sound, 47–50
Sponges, experiments
  with, 30–31, 34–35
Standing (stationary)
  waves, 70–72
Stereos, 41, 57–58
Sticks, experiments
  with, 36–37
Strawberry, Darryl, 50
Straws, experiments
  with, 78–79
Stringed instruments,
  72–75, 83
Submarines, 56–57
Subsonic sounds, 63
Supersonic transport
  (SST), 50
Suppliers, list of, 87–89
Sympathetic vibrations,
  81, 83

Telephones (string and
  tin can), 33
Temperature, effect on
  sound, 52–53
Theaters, acoustics in,
  68–70
Three Matchbox Monte
  trick, 43–44

Thunder, 49
Timing echoes, 55–56
Tone, 60
Toothpick Pulse Meter
  trick, 25
Transverse waves,
  defined, 29
Tubes, experiments
  with, 27–28, 76–77
Tuning forks,
  experiments with,
  24–25, 26, 85–86

Ultrasonic sounds, 63

Vacuums, sound waves
  in, 37, 57
Vibrations (sound)
  cycles of, 58–59
  experiments in,
    23–28
  forced, 83–86
Voice, experiments
  with, 27–28

Water, waves in, 29–31
Wavelength, 58–59
Waves, defined, 29–30
Waves, standing, 70–72
Waves (sound)
  concentrating, 47
  experiments with,
    32–40
  frequency, 58–59
  spread of, 31–32

Waves (water)
    experiments with, 29–31

Whips, 51–52
Wind instruments, 75–79

ABOUT THE AUTHOR

Bob Friedhoffer has been an active, professional magician for over twenty years, performing all over the world in various places such as universities, comedy clubs, nightclubs, libraries, museums, and truly prestigious venues such as the White House in Washington, D.C. His extensive traveling as a performer and author still takes him all over the world, though currently he is devoting much of his time to performing his live science/magic show at many schools and museums in the United States.

Though his University of Miami degree is a BBA in accounting, Mr. Friedhoffer's studies as an undergraduate involved numerous science courses. He is currently finishing up a Master's program at City University of New York entitled Science and Society.

Seymour School Library
East Granby, Conn.

Seymour School Library
East Granby, Conn.

Seymour School Library
East Granby, Conn.